MOM
MILESTONES
The TRUE Story of the First Seven Years

Library of Congress Cataloging-in-Publication Data is available.

ISBN 978-1-5235-1147-1

Workman books are available at special discounts when purchased in bulk for premiums and sales promotions as well as for fundraising or educational use. Special editions or book excerpts can also be created to specification. For details, contact the Special Sales Director at specialmarkets@workman.com.

Workman Publishing Co., Inc.
225 Varick Street
New York, NY 10014-4381

workman.com

WORKMAN is a registered trademark of Workman Publishing Co., Inc.

Printed in China on responsibly sourced paper.
First printing February 2022

10 9 8 7 6 5 4 3 2 1

for my mom

Contents

Note to the Reader

When I became a mother, I was unprepared for how isolating and lonely motherhood would be. It wasn't until I started drawing mom comics that I discovered how universal many aspects of mom life actually are.

The sticky surfaces, the midnight emergency laundry scenarios, the guilt over what's for dinner: We've all been there.

I hope this book comforts you after a rough bedtime or an early wake-up, or any other time.

notes I would send to myself before baby was born

TRAVEL IF YOU GET A CHANCE.

ENJOY A LEISURELY MEAL.

Research mom groups you might want to join.

It's going to be ROUGH but you can do it!

Prologue

Before Mom
Was Born

Before Mom Was Born

She had some hobbies.

She got her hair cut occasionally.

So when are you due?

 LIKES

 taking her time with meals

 reading novels

 perusing cool shops

DISLIKES

 heavy bags or overflowing purses

 not sleeping well

WEEKEND LADY

(BEFORE BABY)

She might browse a bookstore.

She's going to meet up with a friend after 8 p.m.

She might try a new exercise class.

She's going to relax and sleep in!

What mom did to prepare for baby

spent hours researching cute mobiles

read books about birth

bought a bunch of pillows in order to try to sleep

What mom should have done to prepare for baby

bought some comfy pajamas for herself

stocked up on fun reads for long nights

got coffee with friends

BIRTH PLAN: How I thought it would go

WATER BREAKS IN A HILARIOUS WAY

MAD RUSH TO HOSPITAL

PARTNER FAINTS AS BABY IS BORN

SUPER ATTRACTIVE DOCTOR SAYS SOMETHING

notes I would send to myself as a newborn mom

Are you feeling TIRED YET?

Okay, this baby who stays up ALL NIGHT? When he's 8 years old, you will have to play music to get him out of bed in the morning.

Just text that mom you met at the coffee shop! She's lonely too!

This goes by so fast, I promise.

Who knew feeding a BABY would be so complicated?

Chapter One

Newborn Mom

The newborn mom period
is generally thought to
last from day one to
six weeks.

At this stage,
newborn mom may
be able to gaze at
the baby, possibly
with a confused or
bewildered look.

BABY GIRL

Newborn Mom
Nervous System Anatomy

Note: Every mom is different. Some of these nerves may be more or less prominent in different moms.

Brain: responsible for waking up when baby wakes up

Arm nerves: fried after lots of swaying with baby

Cardiac innervation: nerves that pinch at random things (for example, emotional commercials)

Pelvic nerves: still reeling!

Leg nerves: for taking walks

One Day Old

Mom may feel like she is learning a new language. She might be learning to inhabit a new body.

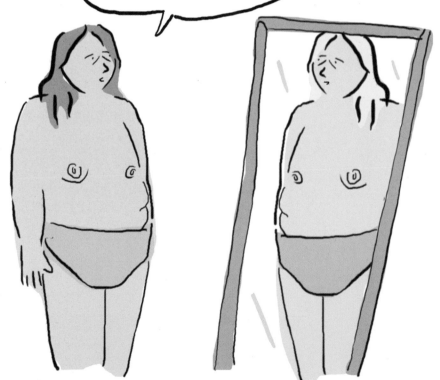

snuggles

skin-to-skin
contact

Drinking
lots of
fluids

Dislikes

wrangling
the
swaddle

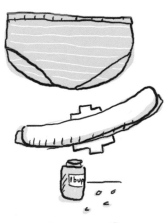

some
physical
realities

The New Vocabulary

flange:
the plastic
part of a
breast pump
that cups
the breast

swaddle:
a soft blanket
used to tightly
wrap a squealing
newborn

**baby gym/
activity center:**
a mat where
baby can "play"

clusterfeed:
when a hungry
newborn wants
to eat for hours

SUPERHEROES
OF THE NEWBORN DAYS

the lactation
Consultant

the delivery
person

the new aunt

the hospital
hurses

Decoding Newborn Sounds

snssshsnhsh

the snarfle:
still sleeping

snsssh SASH

the micro-
snarfle:
waking up

ZZZZZZZZ

loud snore:
sleeping

ZZZZZZZZ

the lawn mower:
sleeping loudly

Pftht

the possible
burp:
baby's first
words

Eeeeee EEE
EEEEE

the cry:
baby's awake!

Things to Contemplate at 3 a.m.

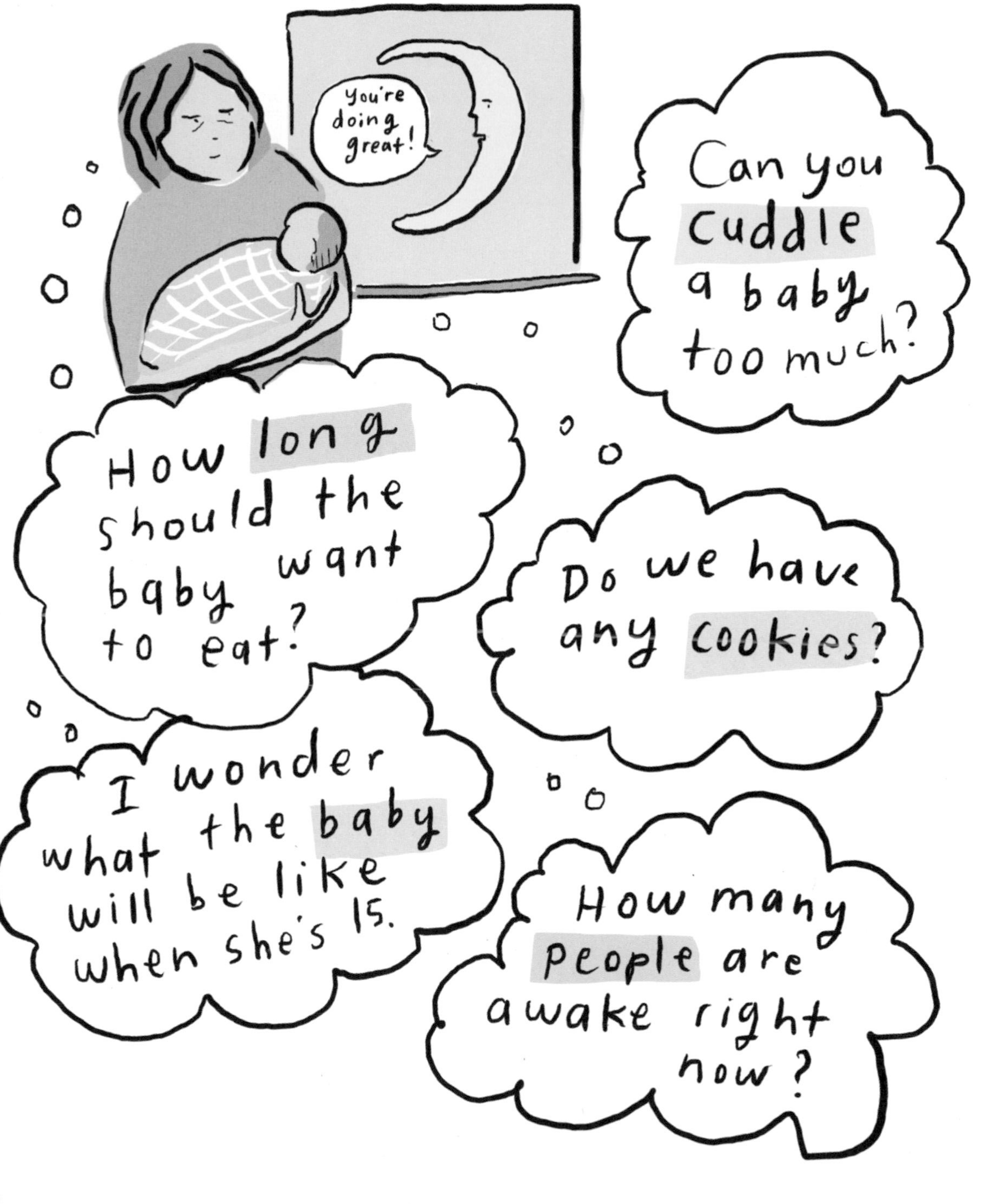

what to bring a
new mom

cookies

something
with
melted
cheese

a salad

a bottle of
wine or
kombucha

an enthusiasm
for doing the
dishes on
her behalf

a little
baggie
of extra
sleep

an interest
in her
birth or
adoption
story

easy-to-put-on
doll clothes
that are actually
for human babies

some
ice
cream

Weekend Mom
OF A NEWBORN

She might try to figure out which newborn onesies still fit!

She may cry in the bathroom.

She will check the diaper bag to make sure there are diapers left.

She will probably do an internet search on newborn sleep.

Two Weeks Old

Mom is likely very tired. Like, more tired than she ever imagined she could be.

mom may start ordering all sorts of things online all night long. (Don't worry, this phase won't last forever.)

Likes

when someone drops off food

Sleeping for more than an hour

-sniff-

the smell of baby's head

Dislikes

Is the baby cold?

unsolicited advice

Skills Learned

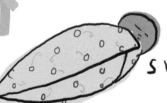

how to swaddle

Swaddling Tips

①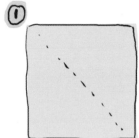

Fold muslin blankie into a **triangle**.

②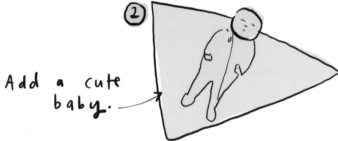

Add a cute baby. →

③ Fold one corner across.

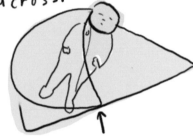

KEY POINT!!
Tuck this tip under baby's bottom to secure it.

④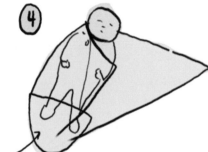

Fold up the tip.

⑤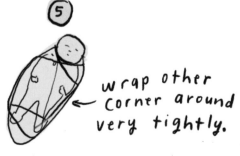

← wrap other corner around very tightly.

⑥ **Ta-da!!**

waaaa

Things a Partner Can Do
(cut this out and post)

- Slice an apple very thinly and present on a nice plate

- Order takeout

- Water the plants

- Do the laundry

Infant Fashion Terms

Onesie

Bubble

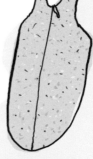

Sleep sack

Robe-style top

Romper

Mitts

"Expert" Newborn Sleep Advice

the mother-in-law

the celebrity doctor

the neighbor

Is this okay?

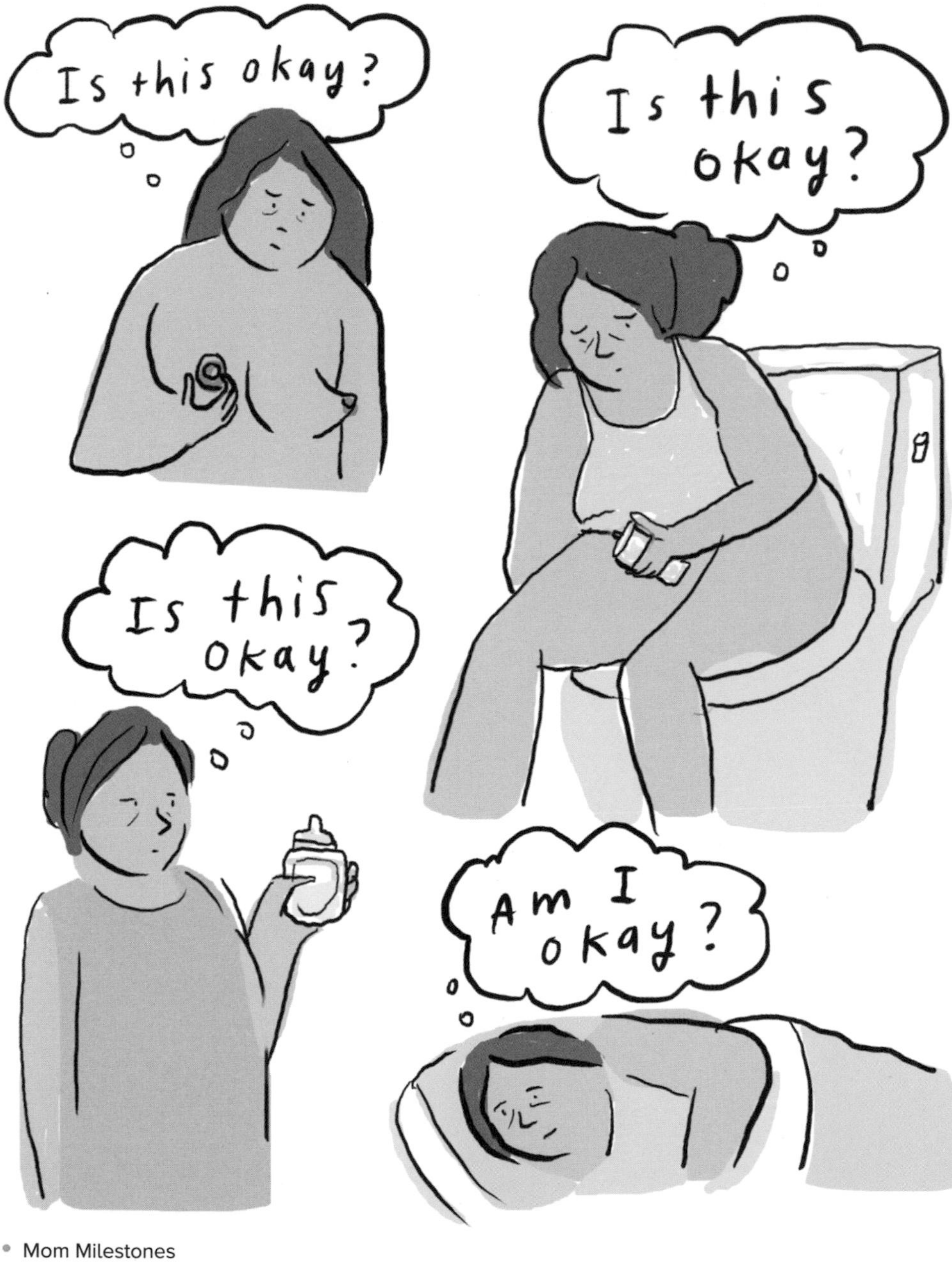

Newborn Momsters

Six Weeks Old

mom may have become really good at writing thank-you notes (even if she chafes at the idea that someone who's just given birth should write thank-you notes).

♥

mom might feel like she's been a mother forever! In fact, she's probably given another mom advice already.

Likes

hot showers

dancing with baby

Dislikes

writing thank-you notes

muscle aches

skills learned

how to soothe baby (sometimes)

places to go with a new baby

the bathroom!

the living room

the window

the mailbox

Leaving the house with baby

Change baby → Feed baby →

Shower Mom

Check weather outside ← Pack diaper bag

Put baby in stroller → Baby Crying

waaaaa

Does baby need a diaper change?

the sweatpants
queen

the NICU
mom

the twin mom

mom Friends you Will Meet

you want the rumble seat...

the one who has done tons of online research

the one already training for a half-marathon

He sleeps for ten hours at night.

the one with the dream baby

Ten Weeks Old

mom has probably joined some virtual mom groups and may be contemplating IRL mom groups.

mom may start to think about childcare if she is getting near the end of her maternity leave.

Mom groups:

mom and baby yoga

lactation support

what are the options?

through the neighborhood

on the internet

- Moms of winter babies
  2,000+ members
- Single Moms Rule
  4+ new posts
  3,000+ members
- Mamas who RUN!
  1500 memb.

Icebreakers for new Moms

newborn mom expressions

phrase	secret meaning
"The baby slept well!"	Baby slept three hours and I am tired.
"we are going out and about."	I am so tired, but we are leaving the couch.
"This is such a special time."	I am so tired.
"The days are long, but the years are short."	will I always be so tired?

EXCERPTS FROM THE MOM MESSAGE BOARDS

3:00 a.m.
Lost our last
pacifier!!!
HALP!!

3:15 a.m.
Similar situation
here. Cluster nursing
now. Send coffee.

3:22 a.m.
WHERE ARE THE CLEAN BOTTLES ???

3:25 a.m.
This baby is an angel during the day but a DEVIL at night!

3:40 a.m.
Sleep when the baby sleeps! Yeah right! Guess I'll sleep at my gynecology appointment then.

4:00 a.m.
Gotta change into my day pajamas now. Baby just spit up.

Twelve Weeks Old

Mom may be returning to her job. Or she might stay home. She may experience a mixed bag of emotions.

curiosity

ELatiON

INEVITABILITY

DREAD

Why is it called a "three-month maternity leave" when 12 weeks is two and a half months?

FEAR

HUNGER

LOGISTICS

FATIGUE

PRIDE!

dehydration

reconnecting with
pre-baby self

Dislikes

WAAAAA

the idea that part of her
heart is external and out
in the world somewhere

Skills Learned

how to leave baby
for periods of time

ALL THE THINGS THAT NEED TO BE ARRANGED IN ORDER TO RETURN TO

work

childcare

work bag

bottles

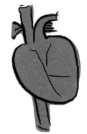

repair broken heart

rediscover work wardrobe and supplement with maternity clothes

MATERNITY CLOTHES:

THE COMEBACK TOUR!

BEFORE BABY

AFTER BABY

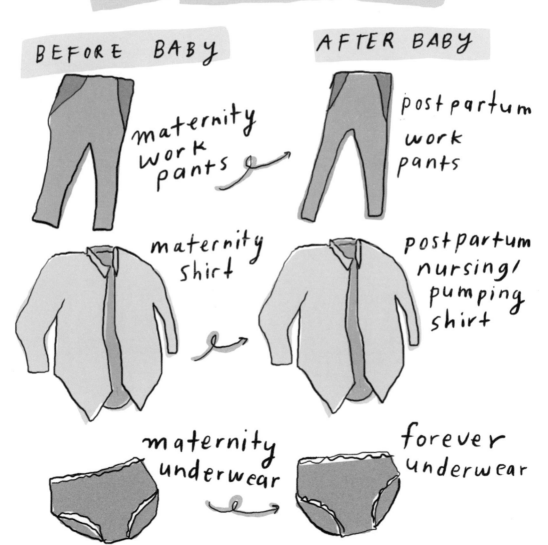

maternity work pants

postpartum work pants

maternity shirt

postpartum nursing/ pumping shirt

maternity underwear

forever underwear

PROS and

OF RETURNING

eating lunch at your own pace

conversations with other adults

feeling very grateful when you get home

CONS

TO WORK AFTER BABY

missing baby

worrying about childcare

feeling very guilty when you get home

sleep when your baby sleeps

IN THE CAR

AT A DINNER PARTY

AT A RESTAURANT OR BAR

WHILE YOU DRY YOUR HAIR

A Letter to You

If you are reading this in the middle of the night

while trying to comfort a newborn,

know that all over the world, other parents are, too.

Have a glass of water, maybe a cookie? Or an apple? (For energy.)

And know that the intense sleep deprivation will end.

And one day (if you're lucky!), the baby will say to you:

"That's not the show I wanted."

notes I would send to myself as an infant mom

SETTING UP CHILD CARE IS A **BEAST. YOU ARE DOING GREAT.**

xoxo Future you

GOLD STAR FOR EFFORT.

As much as you can, surround yourself (physically OR electronically) with many smart moms.

Can you believe how fast this is going? Time is truly an illusion.

Chapter Two

Infant Mom

Mom is now the mother of an infant and may have a PhD in baby sleep.

She may throw around phrases like:

Four-month sleep regression and ... overstimulated

At this stage, mom should be familiar with tummy time.

Infant Mom
NECK MUSCLE ANATOMY

trapezius muscle of lying on the floor

posterior sleep training muscle

the lullaby flexor

the jaw clencher

the carotid artery of tenderness

the blow-out muscle

the jugular vein of childcare guilt

Four months old

Mom is probably getting really good at multitasking.

texting partner

feeding baby

ordering takeout

writing thank-you notes

This is probably the last time mom will only have three toys.

z z z

baby has started
to sleep for longer
stretches

baby smiles

Dislikes

2 a.m. wake-ups,
tripping on baby
gear in the
middle of
the night

Oof

WAAAA

Types of Mom Sleep Regressions

when mom binge-watches three seasons of a show while baby sleeps on her

when mom is awake all night pondering childcare

when mom should go to bed but stays up late reading

when mom falls asleep at 5 p.m.

Things That Can Be Overstimulating for Babies

too much noise

You need a nap.

not enough sleep

You seem calmer now.

staying inside for too long

So I think that exceeds my copay...

listening to mom argue with health insurance companies on the phone

Signs ~~baby~~ MOM might be OVERSTIMULATED

She drank too much coffee.

I can't find my sunglasses!

She keeps asking where her sunglasses are, but she's wearing them.

She was awake for too long last night.

TECH SUPPORT

Q: How many photos will I take? How much RAM does my phone need?

A: Maybe 1,000 photos in the first 100 days?

Q: Do I really need a sound machine?

A: Probably not. A regular speaker is okay.

Q: Is a robot bassinet that comforts baby worth it?

A: Only you can decide...

Seven Months Old

Mom has so much baby gear now.

Likes

Say cheese!

taking pictures of baby

walks with baby

Dislikes

Oh no! No diapers!

an empty diaper bag

Skills Learned

to always carry a snack

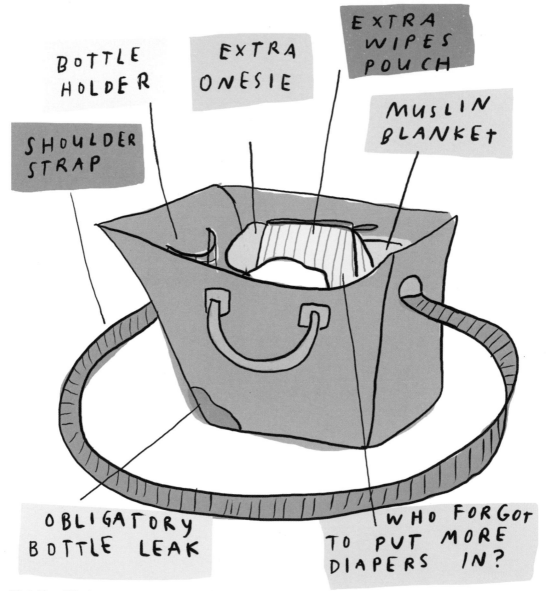

ANATOMY
of a
DIAPER BAG

SHOULDER STRAP

BOTTLE HOLDER

EXTRA ONESIE

EXTRA WIPES POUCH

MUSLIN BLANKET

OBLIGATORY BOTTLE LEAK

WHO FORGOT TO PUT MORE DIAPERS IN?

Which diaper bag is right for you?

the no-nonsense canvas tote

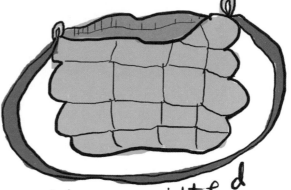

the quilted nylon miracle that carries a dozen diapers

a sleek clutch: one diaper, two wipes, so much hubris

a roomy messenger bag that recalls your youth

First time staying in a hotel room with baby
Well, it's 7 p.m. We could either go to sleep or watch a movie in the bathroom...

Trip with Baby Checklist

- [ ] pajamas (footie)
- [ ] pajamas for day
- [ ] jacket for baby
- [ ] chewy giraffe toy
- [ ] clip-on high chair
- [x] travel crib
- [ ] travel crib linens
- [ ] bottles/sippy cups
- [ ] diapers
- [ ] day clothes
- [ ] hat
- [ ] baby sunscreen?
- [ ] pacifiers
- [ ] sound machine/speaker
- [ ] baby gym?
- [x] swaddles
- [ ] baby snacks/pouches
- [ ] wipes!!! don't forget wipes!
- [ ] mom's stuff

DIAPER WIPES
Sensitive Skin

WEEKEND

Mom of an INFANT

She might read a baby sign language book or article.

She will launder some rompers!

She will wash some bottles.

She might have some "me time" at the pharmacy.

Nine Months Old

Mom is getting old! Mom may have started to chase the baby around.

mom ~~may be~~ is (hopefully) getting more sleep.

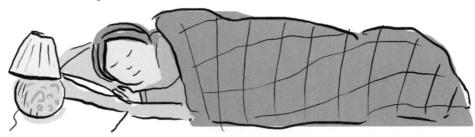

places baby might hide

under the couch

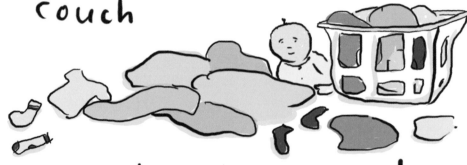

in the laundry

near the toilet paper

That Feeling When You Sleep for More Than Five Hours in a Row for the First Time as a New Mom

Holidays

notes I would send to myself as a toddler mom

Toddlers are EXHAUSTING! Always leaving bananas on the rug and trying to run into the streets!

It won't always require this many BABY WIPES.

It's okay if you don't LOVE this stage of parenting.

GO, MOM, GO!

EVERYTHING IS A PHASE.

Chapter Three

Toddler Mom

now that the baby is a
year old, mom is a toddler
mother!

where did
the time
go?!

Photo
Album

memories of the newborn
stage are slipping away faster
than a toddler can pull a very
loud wooden alligator toy.

Clackety
clackety

Clackety

Clackety

TODDLER MOM
DIGESTIVE TRACT ANATOMY

mouth:
describes
how marvelous
everything
tastes

esophagus:
periodically
feels
choked up
with
emotions

liver:
sometimes
needed
after
a long
bedtime
and a
glass of
wine

stomach:
container
for all
blueberries
and
chicken
nuggets
that child
declines

**small
intestine:**
processes
child's
discarded
veggies

rectum:
rarely allowed
to operate without
an audience

Likes

looking back on the past year

Dislikes

Oh my! This is too small!

baby growing up so quickly

First birthday celebration

birthday parties:
core tenets

EVERYTHING IS OPTIONAL

the cake, the decorations;
even choosing to have
a party is optional.

CELEBRATIONS CAN TAKE MANY FORMS

muffins in lieu of
cake? Sure!

A FIRST BIRTHDAY CAN BE EMOTIONAL

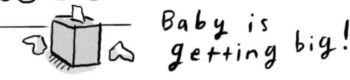

Baby is
getting big!

ANATOMY OF A FIRST BIRTHDAY CAKE

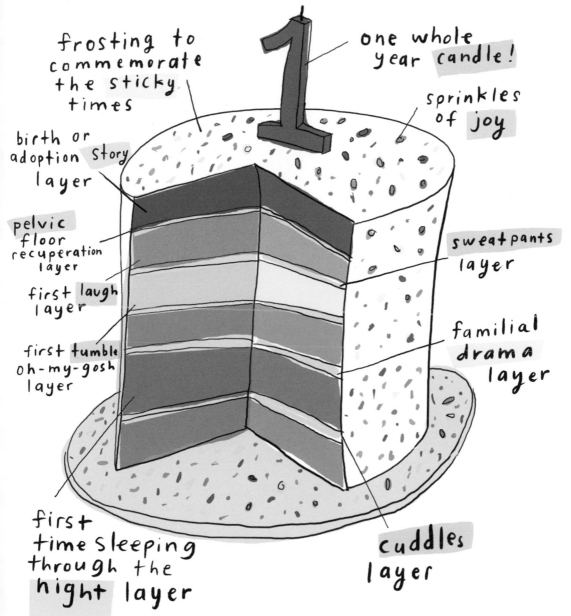

frosting to commemorate the sticky times

one whole year candle!

sprinkles of joy

birth or adoption story layer

pelvic floor recuperation layer

first laugh layer

first tumble oh-my-gosh layer

sweatpants layer

familial drama layer

first time sleeping through the night layer

cuddles layer

What just happened?

looking back at the first year

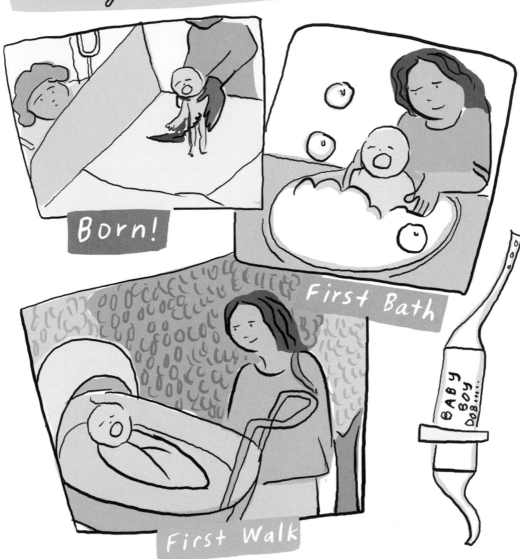

Born!

First Bath

First Walk

First Coffee Shop

Shots

First Food

many Cuddles

Dictionary Entry of Baby's "First" Words

"Ahhh" (verb)
signals an appreciation of music or food

"Baaaa" (noun)
Either means book or bath

"Cacacacaca" (noun)
Said emphatically any time cookies are nearby

"Iiiiii" (noun)
May just be a shriek or it means ice

"Mamamamama" (proper noun)
Definitely means mom! It is not just baby experimenting with their tongue.

Fifteen Months Old

Mom has grown more accustomed to the unrelenting rhythms of motherhood.

She enjoys seeing baby learn new skills.

things strangers say to moms

Glorious things moms like to do alone

GO SHOPPING

GO TO THE POST OFFICE

"RUN ERRANDS"

HIDE IN THE BATHROOM

WORK THINGS

BABYSIT A FRIEND'S NEWBORN

LISTEN TO A PODCAST WITHOUT INTERRUPTION

ORDER DIAPERS ONLINE WHEN ONLY TWO ARE LEFT

Weekend Mom
OF A TODDLER

She might check out a new playground.

She's going to donate the baby clothes (maybe).

She might have a cup of tea.

She will run the dishwasher.

She might go to the playground again.

c'est bon

car seat parts

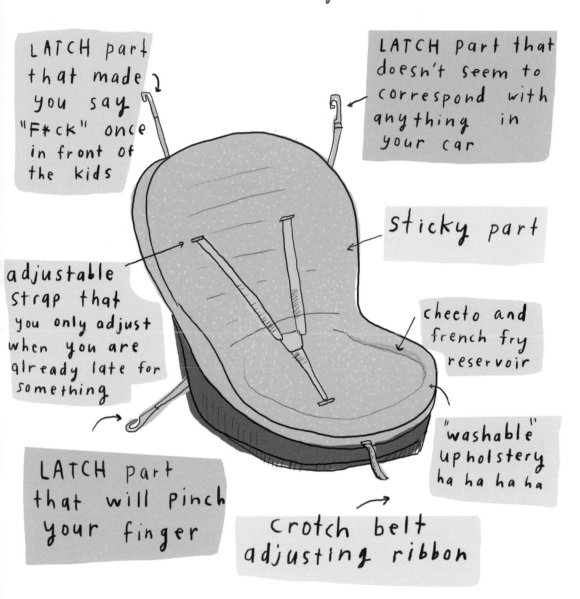

LATCH part that made you say "F*ck" once in front of the kids

LATCH part that doesn't seem to correspond with anything in your car

sticky part

adjustable strap that you only adjust when you are already late for something

cheeto and french fry reservoir

"washable" upholstery ha ha ha ha

LATCH part that will pinch your finger

crotch belt adjusting ribbon

Eighteen months old

Mom enjoys spending time outside with baby.

Likes baby's emerging personality

Zoom Zzzoom

Dislikes baby trying to climb everything

Skills Learned recognizing that a quiet toddler is trouble

PLAYGROUND GAMES
for Mom

Count the number of abandoned kid socks.

Play "would I wear that toddler's outfit if it came in adult sizes?"

maze

start

tantrum

snack time

BAND-AID

GO HOME

the evergreen game of "WHAT IS THAT MOM'S NAME AGAIN?!"

Hiii...

· WORD SEARCH·

```
B  A  B  y  X  M        Baby
O  M  A  U  F  I        Bored
R  O  O  M  D  R        Mama
E  M  R  M  A  A        Mom
D  I  P  E  D  C        Dipe
R  C  I  I  B  L        Nap
N  A  P  F  Q  E        Pacifier
                        Dad
                        Miracle
```

matching socks

kid Haircuts

So many snippets of hair. So many memories. Time slipping through my fingers like tendrils of baby hair...

Toddler

tasting menu
Seven courses

1. mystery course
   (refused sight
        unseen)

2. a stick of string cheese

3. one slice kiwi

4. one quarter banana

— break for tantrum —

5. one almond

6. one applesauce packet

7. one cookie

bon appétit!

Place Settings for Toddlers

no dessert spoon

toy knife

bread plate

water glass

grape juice

mom's wine

banging spoon

what is a napkin?

raisin fork

milk for spilling

saucer

macaroni and cheese fork

throwing fork

yogurt spoon

who put a knife here?!

fruit salad plate

"I no like!" dinner plate

At this age, mom has a robust roster of lullabies that she deploys at bedtime.

sometimes the lullabies work...

lullaby updates

This lil' pig went to market
This lil' pig went home
This lil' pig had pizza
This lil' pig had none
And this lil' pig went
   waaa all the way home.

A, B, C, D, E, F, G, H,
I think my arm
has fallen asleep.

This old mom, she plays one
She plays one on her old
phone with a knick knack
paddy whack, give back
   a mom her phone, this
   old mom keeps rolling home.

If you're tired and you
   know it, close your eyes
If you're tired and you
   know it, close your eyes
etc., etc., ...

The wheels on the
dream bus go
Swishhhh...

Oh my darlin'
Oh my darlin'
Oh my darlin' SLEEPYHEAD
you are getting very sleepy
Oh my darlin' SLEEPYHEAD.

How to stay awake while putting a toddler to sleep

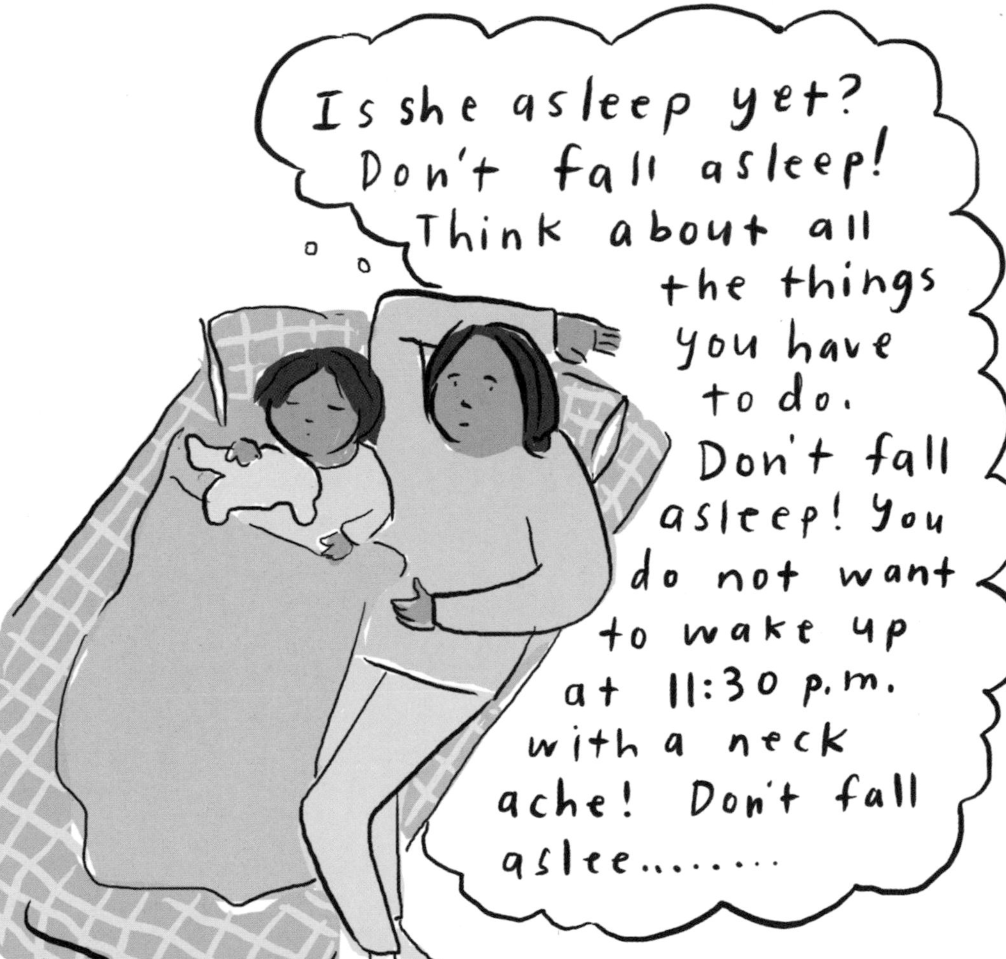

Nap Types

HYPOTHETICAL

UNEXPECTEDLY AND POSSIBLY SICK

RESISTANT

the DOUBLE TROUBLE

nightly routine:
core elements

Find the favorite pajamas.

kiss all the stuffed animals.

Try to read some books
and sing some songs.

Field various snack requests.

BEDTime
THE BOARD GAME

May the odds be in your favor!

EMERGENCY!
BRING SNACK and SKIP NEXT TURN

Where is ? Go back 2

Forgot to brush teeth

Back Rub

Final Song

FIN!

LULLABY TIME

Llama llama NO MORE drama

We are not reading seek and Find (Go back 1)

PICK A BOOK PLEASE

Do NOT horse around in the bathroom!

START:

It's bedtime. I'm starting a BATH.

Two and a half years old

Mom may find that the Terrible Twos are actually a misnomer and it should be the Terrific Twos.

I wuv you!

But there are still tantrums to navigate, as well as the dreaded <u>screen time</u>.

SCREEN TIME!!

MITIGATION

GET SOME FRESH AIR
She'll feel better outside... I think...
WAAAAAAAAAAAA
BATHTIME!
Okay, I'm starting a bath.
WAAAAAAA

SCREEN TIME FEELINGS

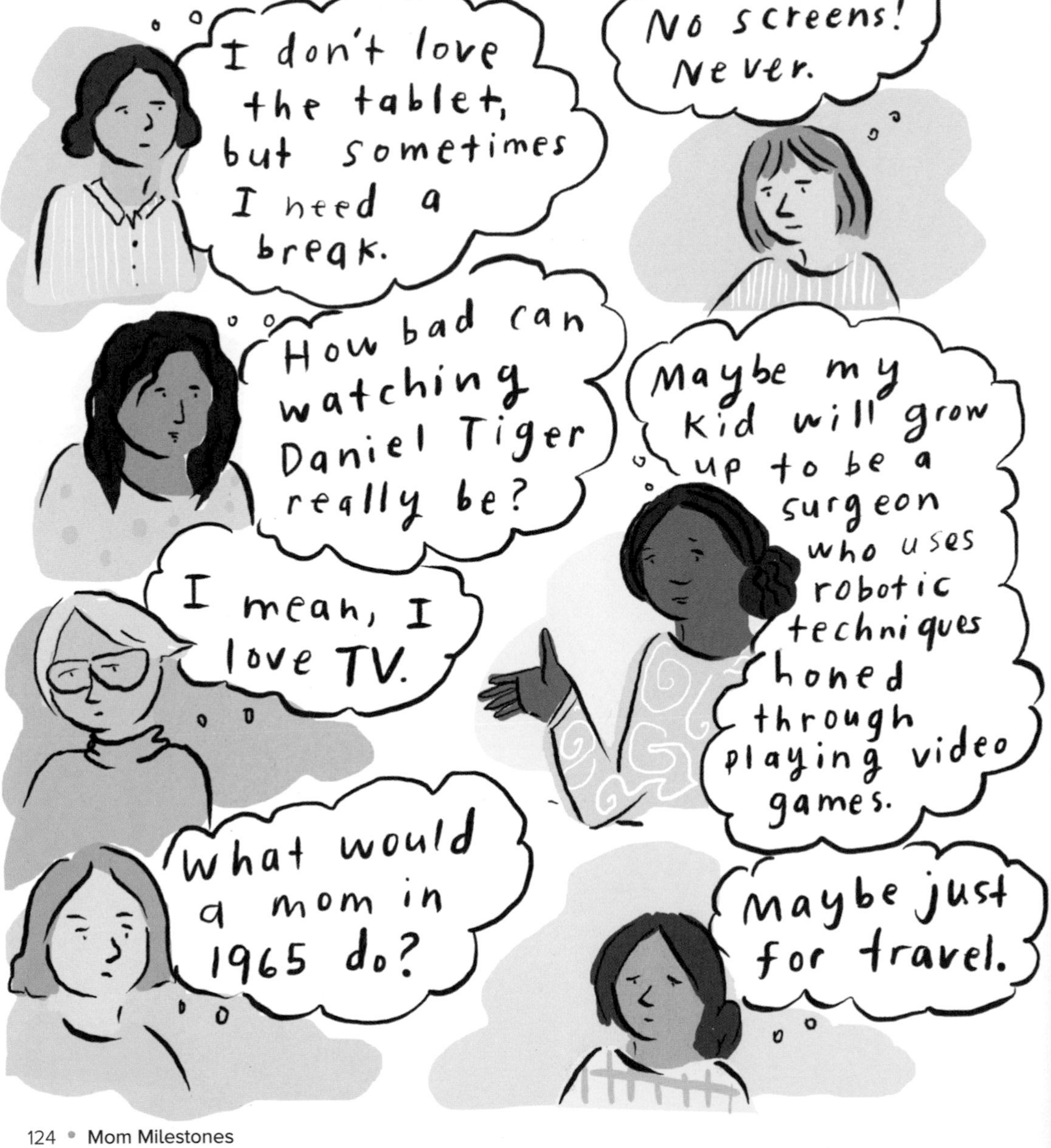

Toddler Brain Anatomy

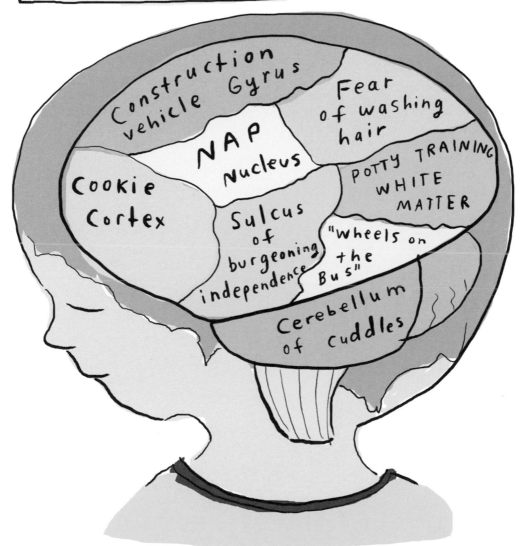

"GREAT" PARENTING BOOKS

The Ultimate Parenting Book by A Doctor Who Never Had Kids

SLEEP TRAIN YOUR BABY by this NEURO-SCIENTIST & Dad

Carefree mothering by a FUN DAD & psychologist

Motherhood: A GUIDE by two physician dads

How Moms Can Raise Better Kids by an Expert

Mom Tantrums: A Guide

Type	Trigger	Treatment
 Caffeine withdrawal Headache	Running out of milk for coffee	Splurge at coffee shop
 Childcare overwhelm	kid gets pink eye and is sent home from preschool	 Put on a movie and call in sick to work
 I can't take it! Too much whining, cleaning, cooking	 stepping on a plastic toy	 time-out for mom

notes I would send to myself as a preschool mom

You don't have to be the class mom.

You'll feel better if you go outside and move your body.

Try to carve out some me time.

will this matter in a year?

I love you and I believe in you.

Chapter Four

Preschool
Mom

This age involves both formal and informal learning. Preschool Mom probably knows how to build with blocks now and how to find a comfortable position on the floor.

Ah, the floor again.

Mom sometimes runs an impressive toy hospital, where she regularly resuscitates even the most critically ill toy trains and action figures.

PRESCHOOL MOM HAND ANATOMY

Flexor Retinaculum: holds hands at crosswalks

Flexor carpi radialis: sets five-minute timers

Opponens pollicis: researches playgrounds

Palmaris brevis: sometimes gets tired while playing with blocks

Flexor pollicis brevis: scrolls parenting articles

Flexor Digitorum Profundis: helps slice grapes

Lumbricals: turn the pages of book

Sheath flexor tendons: rub backs at bedtime

Three Years Old

Mom might have already had another kid, or is considering it, or is very grateful for just the one.

Mom is now acquainted with many childhood illnesses.

kid art

preschoolers
in cardigans

Dislikes

all things
potty training

Skills Learned

how to coax a kid
into taking
medicine

When did we accumulate so many TOYS?

loud clackety alligator

xylophone

shape sorter

musical school bus

stuffed animals

plastic maracas

Ditching the Pacifier aka binky

Stages of Bathtime

Stage 1:

Refusal

Stage 2:

Enjoyment

Stage 3:

Endless Bath

things moms do during bathtime

READ NOVELS

FOLD LAUNDRY

MAKE MENTAL CHECKLISTS

- Dentist
- Kid dentist
- OB-GYN
- Pediatrician
- Car inspection
- Birthday plans
- Milk

RELAX

Three and a half years old

Mom may be an expert on children's books now.

Let's do something that doesn't involve tacos or dragons tonight.

She may be very good at packing lunches for preschool.

Likes watching kids make friends

Dislikes emptying the lunchbox with mystery smells

Things preschoolers do

Creep up silently and scare the living daylights out of you

Turn nouns into marvelous verbs

Ask ontological questions

Need cuddles in the middle of the night

Preschool horrors

uncapped
Play-Doh
containers

Oh nooo!

losing an
object of
significance

realizing it's
your turn for
snack day and
you need 12
clementines and
cheese sticks

WEEKEND MOM
of a PRESCHOOLER

She might look up fun crafts online.

She's going to peel a tangerine.

She might get some new bedtime stories at the library.

She would like to take a "nice walk."

She might try to match up all the orphaned, unmatched socks.

Weekend F.A.Q.

Question	Answer
Will you put on "No" by Meghan Trainor? *No no no*	Yes, but not before 10 a.m. and only once per 24-hour period. *No no No No*
CAN I HAVE A SNACK?	Please help yourself to an apple or a carrot.
Can I have a bubbly water?	No, those are expensive. Okay, fine, never mind, I'm just grumpy.
Where are the scissors and tape?	Maybe where you left them.

Mom's Best Approaches to Feeding Kids

"Eat the Rainbow"

Here is a colorfu—

Can I have a cookie?

Focus on *Nutrition*

Does anyone want a PROTEIN snack? Or a HEALTHY fat?

Entirely POUCH-based

Apple Sauce

Banana

Carrot &

Broccoli

PEACH

Things Parents Do at 6 a.m.

run the laundry

empty the dishwasher

search for stuff

hide the xylophone

set a timer for five more minutes

desperately charge the tablet

take some ibuprofen

make the coffee

other "siblings"

Pets

Day care buddies

Cousins

Neighbors

Four Years Old

mom occasionally enjoys kid activities but also likes to do her own thing from time to time.

Likes sharing passions with kid

Dislikes sticky spots

Skills Learned how to do a "playdate"

PRESCHOOL DATA PRESENTATION

Figure 1. Scooter Utilization

time spent riding the scooter

time adult spends carrying the scooter

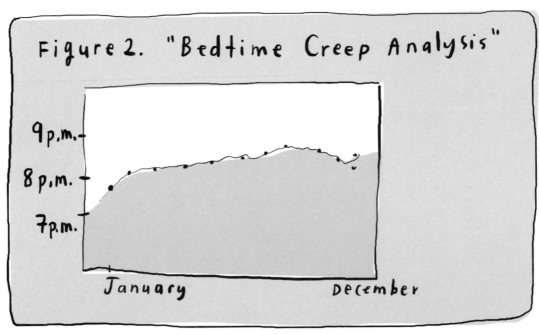

Figure 2. "Bedtime Creep Analysis"

9 p.m.
8 p.m.
7 p.m.

January   December

Figure 3. Cleanup Room Habits

kid cleans up

mom cleans up

babysitter cleans up

no one cleans up

Figure 4. Who Finds Lost Things

kid

mom

dog

Figure 5. Snack Requests

Sunset

Time of Day

Sunrise

Number of Requests

MOM's FAVORITE PHRASES

Let's go move our bodies!

Just a minute...

What's the MAGIC word*?

Let's use kind words.

Has anyone seen the tape?

Aww, I love you so much.

* It's "PLEASE."

T-shirts for Mom

Do you want PIZZA or PB&J?

Wait, I look tired?!

FRONT

Thanks for letting me know.

BACK

Use your LOOKING eyes to find it!

Fun

Do you have an extra hair tie?

If I look tired, it's because I'm not wearing mascara and I am tired.

things to avoid on the day you decide to give away your kid's newborn clothes

OLD PHOTOS OR VIDEOS

THE PILE OF MUSLIN SWADDLES

ANYTHING THAT WILL MAKE YOU MORE EMOTIONAL OR IRRITABLE

ANYTHING THAT SMELLS LIKE A CLEAN DIAPER OR BABY SHAMPOO

Four and a half years old

mom is contemplating school.

she may be trying to introduce colors and letters in a chill way. No pressure!

LIKES

Arts & Crafts!

DISLIKES

ARTS & CRAFTS!!

THE Motherhood

a
applesauce
pouches

b
baby

c
coffee

g
The Giving Tree

H
holding
hands

i
ice cream

m
make-believe

N
night
night

O
ouch!

S
sippy
cup

T
Tablet policy

U
umbrage

Y
yogurts

Z
zoo

Alphabet

D drama

e ennui

f Frozen

J juice boxes

K kindness of strangers

L HA HA HA HA laughter

P pacifier

Q quiet time

r raisins

V vacuum cleaner

W water balloons

X xoxo

more games for moms

IDENTIFY THE SPILLS

1.
2.
3.
4.
5.

A. Orange Juice
B. Water
C. Chocolate milk
D. Red wine
E. Tears

ANSWER KEY
1.C 2.E 3.D 4.B 5.A

STORY TIME! ♫ ♪

Once upon a time, a _____
noun
listened to music from _____
kids' movie
so many times that_____ _____
pronoun   verb (past tense)
and told _____ that they
noun
couldn't _____ again.
verb (present tense)

Categories of kid art

First finger painting

Keep it.

Brown blob stage

Toss it.

Ceramic beast

Take it to the office.

Mixed media

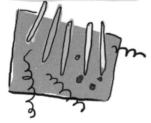

Recycle it.

Self-portrait

Frame it.

Glitter project

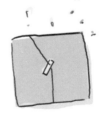

Don't even bring it home!

Chill Crafts with Kids

DRAW ON
ROCKS WITH
PAINT PENS

TAPE TOGETHER
ASSORTED ITEMS
FROM RECYCLING
BOX

COMPARE THE
COLOR AND INTENSITY
OF VARIOUS CRAYONS
ACCUMULATED OVER
THE YEARS

THE ALWAYS
RELIABLE
CARDBOARD
BOX/HOUSE/SHIP/
TIME MACHINE

crafts moms enjoy

 easy cleanup

 nice sentiment

no glitter or glue involved

can be used as a nice grandparent present

done at school

notes I would send
to myself as a
kindergarten mom

kids pick
up on your
ENERGY.

ONE
DAY YOUR
KID WILL
ENJOY
SALADS.

Time
is
precious.

Don't let
ANY slime
enter the
house.

Chapter Five

Kindergarten Mom

Mom has a kindergartner now, and it might be mom's favorite age so far. Her child is still a tiny kid but one with so many thoughts and insights.

Do you know liquids can become gas?

Tomorrow is Pajama Day!

What does "befriend" mean?

Kindergarten Mom
EYE ANATOMY

Sclera: shoe-size confusion

Retina: sees time passing in a BLUR!

Cornea: once scratched by child

Pupil: laser focus on bedtime

Macula: fails to see toys on carpet at night

Iris: Can see kid doing mischievous things in another room

Lens: tries to put phases in perspective

Five Years Old

During marginally successful sit-down meals, mom now tries to extract details about what happened at school.

Your first day of Kindergarten

You might have some BIG FEELINGS.

It might help to set out your clothes the night before.

The teacher is excited to meet you and your family.

Hi!

The first day will go by so fast!

things that are shockingly difficult to teach

TYING SHOELACES

RIDING A BICYCLE

USING UTENSILS

Postcards to

Don't despain!
One day we'll hang
out again!

Love you!

Greetings ☆
from BEDTIME!

We have read
four books, sung five
lullabies, and drunk
one glass of water!

Mom Friends

Thank you for sending me that interesting parenting article.

I'm texting you from the bathroom.

I've locked myself in here.

Let's take a walk soon. ♡

Everything I needed to know I learned as a kindergarten mom

Always pack a snack and a water bottle.

Everyone likes to earn a gold star.

It doesn't hurt to bring a spare change of clothes.

A little glitter goes a long way.

cleanup always goes better with a song.

Offering to share something is a great way to break the ice with new friends.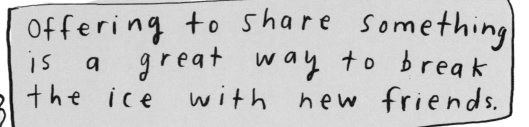

Fresh air is a great reset.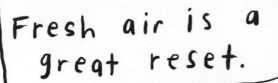

Like Play-Doh, the smallest things can shape and change us.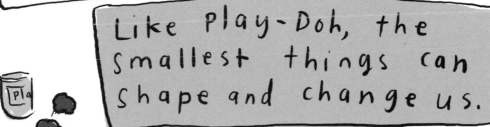

Life is curious and beautiful.

Five and a half years old

Mom may be growing accustomed to the tempo of school and how long it takes to do things.

She has a different kind of Sunday Scaries now.

Likes gathering intelligence from other moms

Dislikes coming up with dinner ideas at 6 p.m.

Skills Learned to throw away the brown Play-Doh

Map of a walk with a Kindergartner

START

Interesting STICK

BATHROOM EMERGENCY

Distracted by a BEE

SNACK BREAK

Snacks deemed TERRIBLE *CRYING*

Sunday Scaries: Mom Edition

Do the kids have any clean clothes for school tomorrow?

Do we have anything for breakfast?

Did I set the alarm?

Is it our turn to bring snacks for 16 kids?

Am I due to see the gynecologist?

The Invisible Chore Chart

Schedule dentist appointments

Teacher Appreciation

Kid needs soccer cleats

VACCINES UP TO DATE?

Try to get kid to READ

Schedule babysitter

getting enough SLEEP?

SUMMER PLANS

eating enough vegetables?

RUN THE DISHWASHER

Mother-in-Law's BIRTHDAY

Dinner Tonight?

Kid's birthday

ME TIME

what's in Mom's Bag?

lipstick applied annually

granola bars in various states of undress

toys in need of repair

napkins that will function as tissues

dental hygiene stuff

something unrecognizable at the bottom

WEEKEND MOM

OF A KINDERGARTNER

Let's all try going to the bathroom ONE LAST TIME before we leave!

She might go on a family bike or scooter ride.

She's going to want "quiet time" after lunch.

She will need to grab some "good bread" at the store.

She might start a fun new book.

notes I would send to myself as an elementary school mom

1st place in worrying

1st

Dear Mom,

Great job reading those four picture books at bedtime.

Love You!

you are so great at keeping track of the water bottles!

DEEP BREATHS

Chapter Six

Elementary School mom

Okay, elementary school just sounds...old! Even though kindergarten is physically in the same place, first grade sounds like it might as well be a PhD program.

elementary school mom
BRAIN ANATOMY

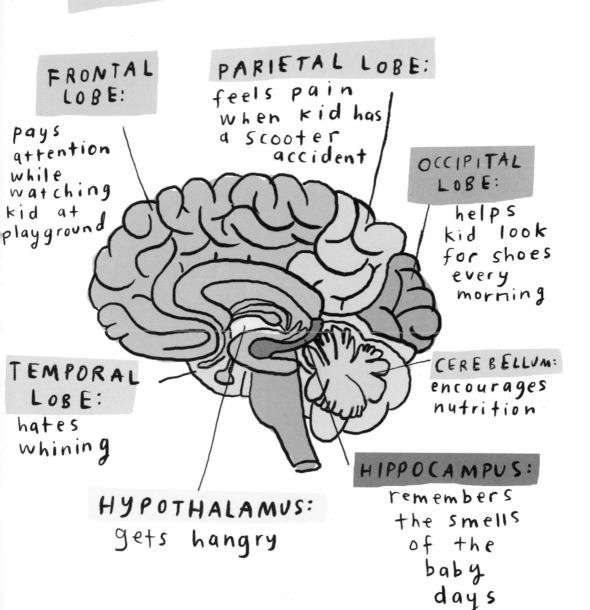

FRONTAL LOBE:
pays attention while watching kid at playground

PARIETAL LOBE:
feels pain when kid has a scooter accident

OCCIPITAL LOBE:
helps kid look for shoes every morning

TEMPORAL LOBE:
hates whining

CEREBELLUM:
encourages nutrition

HYPOTHALAMUS:
gets hangry

HIPPOCAMPUS:
remembers the smells of the baby days

Six Years Old

Mom may be more focused on her kid's independence and may occasionally ask her kid to "play by yourself for a while" or listen to an audiobook.

mom enjoys reading. Did she mention she loves to read?

Likes telling knock-knock jokes, reading longer books together

Dislikes hurt feelings

What happened at school today?

Interrogation Techniques

 Roses, Buds, and Thorns:
One nice thing (rose)
One bad thing (thorn)
One thing you're looking
forward to tomorrow (bud)

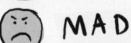 GLAD
 MAD
SAD

Name one thing
about your day
that made you
glad, mad, or sad

Spy Movie Style

Mom Just Blathers About Her Day Until Someone Takes Pity on Her and Tells a Story About Their Day

Mom's Ear Anatomy

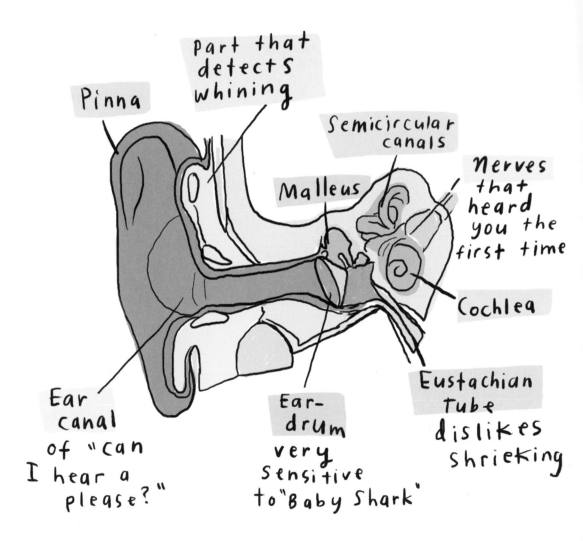

Pinna

Part that detects whining

Semicircular canals

Malleus

Nerves that heard you the first time

Cochlea

Ear canal of "can I hear a please?"

Ear-drum very sensitive to "Baby Shark"

Eustachian Tube dislikes shrieking

Anatomy of a six-year-old's ear

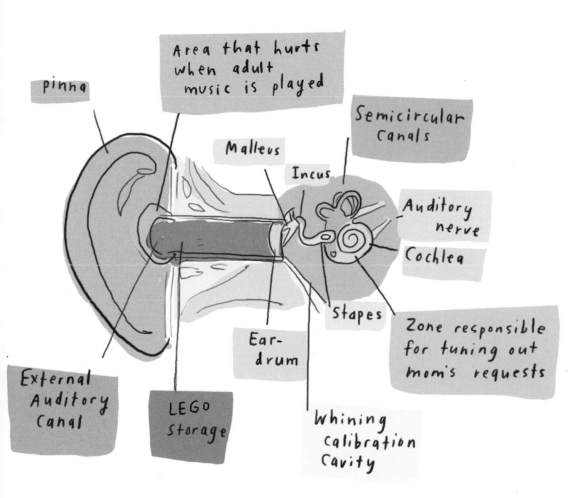

pinna

Area that hurts when adult music is played

Semicircular Canals

Malleus

Incus

Auditory nerve

Cochlea

External Auditory Canal

LEGO Storage

Ear-drum

Stapes

Zone responsible for tuning out mom's requests

Whining calibration cavity

Seven Years Old

mom intermittently does tooth fairy duties.

°° Should I throw this away or should I keep all of the teeth and make them into a necklace to one day present to my kid's future partner?

Other nights she's up thinking about the future. She wants her kid to grow up in a kind and healthy world.

Likes  eating healthy foods, staying active

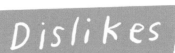

Dislikes requests for video games

Mom, Can I get Super Bug Blast?

Skills Learned

how to have conversations  about hard things

Mother's Day Cards for Mom Friends

You do a mean grilled cheese!

Thanks for talking about pelvic floor physical therapy with me!

YOU ARE THE BEST MOM (FRIEND).

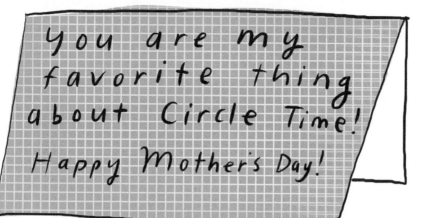

Weekend Mom
of an elementary schooler

She might make banana **bread.**

She might organize all the shoes by the front door.

She might want to connect with nature.

She will want to _____ meal plan for the week.

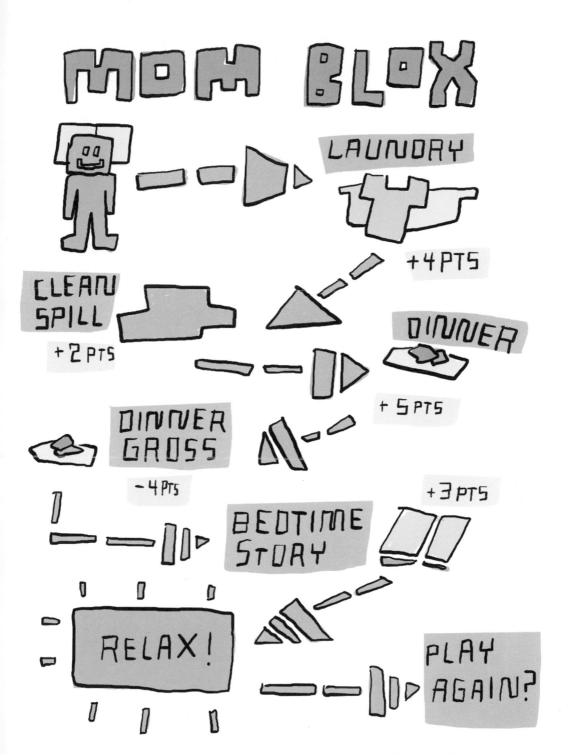

Parenting Report Card

Class	Grade	Comments
Reading	B-	Only wants to read two stories at bedtime.
Science	C+	Minimal effort in reptiles unit.
Art	B+	More focused on "creating a mess" than art process.
Math	A+	Great at counting to 5.
Gym	B	Does not enjoy indoor sports. Multiple requests to "not throw ball inside."

Life with a seven-year-old

Notes I am Sending to My Future Self

GOOD TRY.

Time is precious.

You can trust your instincts here.

PEACE

Epilogue

As Mom Grows Up

Now mom sometimes sees babies at the grocery store and she remembers how challenging those days were.

As she and her kid(s) grow, she knows that there are still challenges, joys, heartbreaks, and snacks ahead. Because that's what motherhood is, right?

Mom's Journey

In case no one mentioned it...

YOU MAKE A GREAT SNACK PLATE

THE WAY YOU LOAD THE DISHWASHER IS PERFECTION

YOU ARE A LAUNDRY MAGICIAN

YOU DESERVE A SMALL BOWL OF NUTS

MOM

Things Mom Has Already Forgotten

when the kids stopped using sippy cups

how **potty** training works

how long the **raisin-** eating period lasted

the date of baby's first **smile**

when they began sleeping through the **night**

when the toy train stage ended

WEEKEND
mom in the Future

She might do some work in the garden.

She might try a new-to-her spice.

She will probably clean the fridge.

She will want to make a meal to take to a new mom.

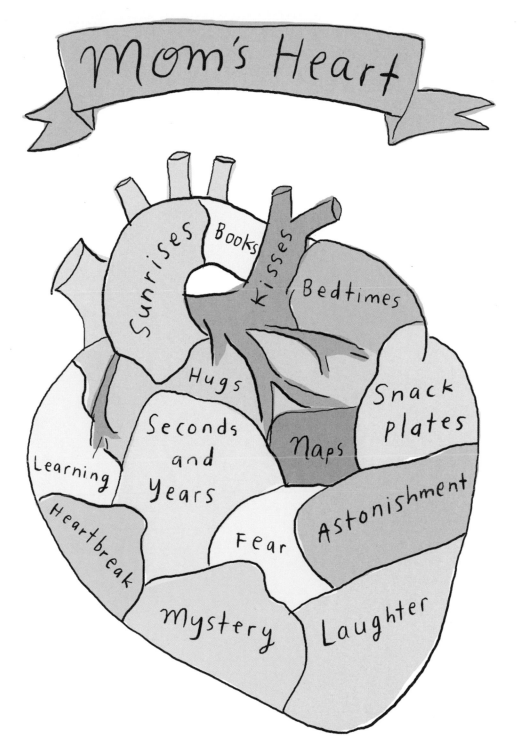

Acknowledgments

 Thanks to all of the busy moms who provided ideas and feedback on this project. Sara, Marisa, Virginia, Amanda, and Ashley: Thank you!

 Thanks Joanna for giving my drawings a home on Cup of Jo. *merci*

 Thanks to Mel Flashman and Lauren Mechling for your book doula services.

Thank you Rachael Mt. Pleasant for the excellent editing! Much thanks to the rest of the Workman team.

Thanks to readers on Instagram who always make me LOL.

Finally, thanks to Arthur, George, Russ, Rachel, Ryan, my mom, and my dad for your love and support.

About the Author

Grace Farris is a mom, doctor, and illustrator.

Her work has appeared in the New York Times, Vogue, BuzzFeed, and Cup of Jo. She lives in Austin, Texas, with her family.

You can find her on Instagram at @coupdegracefarris.